Fixed Income Securities

A beginner's guide to understand, analyze, evaluate and invest in Fixed Income securities

Dr. M. Imran Ahsan Dhothar

Preface

This book is designed to make Fixed Income Securities simple, practical, and valuable for you—whether you are an investor seeking smarter decisions or a learner eager to finally understand this often "complicated" subject.

While there are many books on the market, most either overwhelm with jargon or leave gaps in understanding. This book takes a different path: it delivers the **complete picture** of fixed income analysis in a **clear, concise, and structured** way.

Drawing on my over **ten years of teaching experience as a university instructor**, I have learned how to break down complex ideas into concepts that are not only understandable but also enjoyable to learn. What usually feels like a dry and technical subject will—through this book—feel intuitive and manageable.

My promise is straightforward: **if you give this book a week, you will grasp fixed income securities with confidence.** The language is simple, the flow is logical, and the focus is always on clarity over complexity.

I wish you the best—both in your learning journey and in the investment decisions ahead. And remember, if you face any hurdles, you are welcome to reach out to me directly.

Let's begin.

Ch. Imranahsen@gmail.com

WhatsApp # 00923465006818

Contents

CHAPTER 1: FIXED-INCOME SECURITIES: INTRODUCTION

Basic features of fixed-income securities

The most common type of fixed-income security is a bond. In essence, a bond is a debt instrument in which the issuer promises to make periodic payments to the lender—the investor who purchases the bond—over a specified period of time. The bond issuer acts as the borrower, while the buyer of the bond acts as the lender, providing the capital.

The value of a bond is primarily driven by two factors: prevailing interest rates and the credit risk of the issuer. When interest rates rise, the value of an existing bond falls. This is because its future fixed cash flows are now discounted at a higher rate, making them less valuable in today's terms.

Similarly, the risk of default significantly impacts a bond's price. The higher the perceived risk of the issuer defaulting, the lower the bond's value. To compensate for this additional risk, investors demand a higher potential return, which is achieved by paying a lower price for the bond.

A bond has the following features

- Name of the issuer of the bond
- Maturity date
- Par value (principal value)
- Coupon rate (interest rate to be paid)
- Currency of payments

Issuers of bond: The Following can be the issuer of the bond

Companies: The Financial and non-financial companies issue bonds.

Sovereign governments (countries): Countries also issue treasury bills and other types of bonds.

Non-sovereign governments (municipalities, states, provinces)

Quasi-government entities: Bonds issued by the government-sponsored agencies and entities.

Supranational entities: Global organizations like the European Union, the IMF, etc.

Maturity: The date mentioned on the face of the bond on which the principal amount would be paid back. The period remaining in maturity is called tenor or term to maturity. Bonds with a maturity of less than one year are called **money market instruments**, and bonds with a maturity of more than one year are called **capital market securities.** Some bonds are issued with no maturity and are called *perpetual bonds.* In this type of bond, the principal amount is never paid back, but periodic payments are made forever.

Par value: The principal amount that would be paid at maturity is called par value. It also has different names like face value, maturity value, and redemption value. Face value can be the same as or different **from** the bond price. When a bond is being traded or sold at a price higher than its par value, it is called a premium. When a bond is traded or sold at a price lower than its par value, it is called a discount.. Usually, the price is written (for the first issue) as a percentage of the face value.

Coupon rate: The Coupon rate is the annual percentage rate of the face value. A bond with a face value of $100 and a coupon rate of 10% will pay 10$ annually. Bonds can be annual, semiannual, or quarterly paying. If the coupon rate is 10% in a semiannual bond, it would pay 10%/2 = 5% after six months.

Currency: The currency in which the bond is issued is also mentioned on the bond's face. A *dual-currency bond* is a bond in which the interest is paid in one currency while the principal is to be paid in another currency. A currency-option bond gives the lender an option to choose from two currencies.

Content of a bond indenture

A legal contract between the issuer and buyer of a bond is called a bond indenture or trust deed. Bond indenture specifies the issuer and buyer's responsibilities and the bond's characteristics. The provisions in the bond indentures are called bond covenants. These covenants are positive and negative.

Positive covenants: These are also called affirmative covenants. These are the actions that the borrower (issuer) promises to perform. Affirmative covenants usually include the promise to promptly pay interest and principal amount, maintain a specific asset, and comply with applicable laws.

Negative covenants are the restrictions imposed on the issuer (borrower). These usually include restrictions on the sale or pledging of the same collateral asset and restrictions on additional borrowings. These covenants protect the bondholder's interests and reduce the borrower's default risk.

Legal, regulatory, and tax considerations - issuance and trading of fixed-income securities

The bonds are subject to specific regulatory and tax laws depending on where the bonds are issued, traded, and where the bondholders are.

According to geographic location, bonds can be divided into the following forms.

Domestic bonds: Bonds issued by domestic firms traded in the domestic market in local currency are called domestic bonds. For instance, domestic bonds are traded in the US bond market in USD if a US firm issues bonds.

Foreign bonds: Bonds issued by a firm in another market in foreign currency and traded in that country are referred to as foreign bonds. For example, a US firm issues bonds in China, denominated in Yuan, and they are traded in China and are called foreign bonds.

Eurobonds: Bonds issued internationally, outside the domestic market of any single country, and denominated in a currency other than that of the country where the issuer is primarily located. For example, a Japanese company issuing USD-denominated bonds in London. These bonds are subject to fewer regulations than domestic bonds. These bonds were initially started from Europe, so they are called euro bonds and can be in any currency (not necessarily in euros). Euro bonds are issued in bearer form. A bearer form is one in which the bondholder is the owner. There is no need to register the name of the holder of that bond. The opposite of a bearer bond is a registered bond, in which the holder's name must be registered. Investors who want to avoid taxes hold bearer bonds.

Global bond: When a bond is issued in several countries simultaneously, it is called a global bond. This bond is also not denominated in the issuing country's currency.

Income from these bonds is taxed like other income. The capital gain is also taxed differently in different countries. Capital gain in the short term can be taxed differently or the same way as long-term capital gain. Some bonds, like US municipal bonds, are exempt from tax.

In some jurisdictions, a discounted bond is treated as capital gain and taxed accordingly. Tax treatments also differ depending on whether the bond is at a premium, discount, or par.

Cash flow structures of fixed-income securities

According to the payment structure, bonds can be divided into the following types.

Bullet structured bond/ Bullet bond: This is the most common type of bond. In this bond, the coupon payments are made periodically, and the principal amount is paid at maturity, usually along with the final coupon payment. For example, a 3-year bond with a $100 face value and a coupon payment of 10% annually would pay as follows.

Year	1	2	3
Payment	10	10	110

Fully amortized loan: When the bond pays the periodic coupon plus a proportion of the principal amount periodically, it is called a fully amortized loan. Car and home loans are usually fully amortized loans. This loan is fully amortized with the final payment, with no separate principal amount payment.

Partially amortized loan: This is not a standard fixed-income instrument. In this, some principal amount is amortized and paid with coupon payments periodically, but at maturity, the unamortized amount plus coupon payments are made.

Contingency provisions - timing and/or nature of cash flows of fixed-income securities

Contingency provisions are embedded options for either the issuer or the bondholder. These provisions give the holder and/or issuer some rights to exercise. (A bond with no contingency provisions is called a straight or option-free bond.) Bonds with these embedded options can be callable, puttable, or convertible bonds.

Callable bonds: A Callable bond gives the right of *call option* to the bond issuer. A call option gives the issuer the right to redeem a bond at a specific price on a specific date. It protects the issuer from the risk of declining interest rates. For example, a bond with a 100$ face value and 5% coupon rate can have the following types of call options;

The issuer can redeem the bond at 101% of face value on 21 January 20x3.

The issuer can redeem the bond at 100% of face value on 21 February 20x4.

If the issuer sees a massive decline in interest rate below 5%, he can redeem his bond on these dates. That bond before any redeemable date is called *a call-protected* bond for that period.

Companies also exercise call options (along with a decline in interest rates) because their credit rating has increased and default risk has declined. Now they can issue a new security with a lower coupon rate.

This callable option is not beneficial for the bondholder because it will only be exercised when the market interest rate has fallen, and the investor will not get that much yield on any other instrument in the market. That is why callable bonds are issued with a higher coupon rate than non-callable similar bonds. The difference between callable and non-callable identical bonds equals the value of the call option to the issuer.

A call option can be any of the following types.

American-style call option: The call option can be exercised anytime after the first call date.

European-style call option: Bonds can be called only on a specified date.

Bermuda style call option: Bonds can be called on a specified date after the first call date.

These call prices make up the upper limits of the bond's price.

There is another call provision called the make-whole call provision.

Make-whole call provision: In this call provision, the issuer does not fix the call price, but it is calculated as the present value of the remaining coupon payments of that bond. The present value cannot be lower than the market value of that bond, so the issuer does not exercise this option unless there is an acquisition, merger, or similar type of thing happening with the issuer.

Puttable bonds: The put option gives the bondholder the right to sell the bond back to the issuer at a specific price. Like the call option, a bondholder can only use the put option. Bondholders will exercise the put option if the market or fair value of the bond is less than the put price or the issuer's credit rating has fallen. A puttable bond gives extra rights to bondholders compared to an option-free bond; that is why a puttable bond is sold at higher prices (or with a lower yield) than an option-free bond with similar qualities.

Convertible bond: A convertible bond gives the bondholder the right to convert it into a specific number of common shares. When the market or fair value of the common shares increases, the bondholders can exercise this option. Again, this benefits the bondholder, so the price is higher (lower yield). The convertible bonds are called hybrid securities because of the convertible option into common shares. This gives minimum price protection to bondholders. *Conversion price* is the price at which the bond can be converted into common shares. *Conversion ratio* equals the par value of the bond/conversion price. The **conversion price** is the predetermined price at which the bond can be converted into common shares. The **conversion ratio** is equal to the par value of the bond divided by the conversion price.
The **conversion value** is the market value of the common shares that would be received upon conversion.

Warrants: Warrants are not embedded options. They are given with straight bonds. Warrants give the right to bondholders to buy a company's shares at a given price over time. Warrants attached to bonds are called sweeteners because they make a debt more attractive to the investors (with potential profit addition).

Contingent convertible bonds (CoCos): These are the bonds that will be converted into a specific number of common shares if a particular event occurs. For example, a bond is issued with a condition to maintain a certain level of equity. If the equity falls below the required level, the bonds would be automatically converted into common shares to maintain that required equity level. This conversion will increase the equity and reduce the debt liabilities.

CHAPTER 2: FIXED-INCOME MARKETS

Classifications of global fixed-income markets

The global bond market can be divided with respect to the type of issuer, creditworthiness, maturity of bond, coupon structure, geography of issuance, indexing, and taxability.

Classification with respect to the issuer

There are three bond market sectors in **this** regard: the government and government-related sector, the corporate sector, and the structured (securitized) sector. The **government and government-related sector** includes bonds issued by the federal government, states, municipal corporations, and supranational organizations like **the** World Bank. Corporate bonds are issued by **both** financial corporations and non-financial corporations.

In the case of securitized bonds, different debt products are pooled together to **create** a new security, which is then sold to investors. These bonds are issued by a **Special Purpose Entity (SPE)**, which is created for the purpose of issuing these securities.

Classification with respect to the credibility of the issuer

Credit rating is provided by credit rating agencies like Standard and Poor's (S&P), Moody's, and Fitch. According to S&P and Fitch, AAA, AA, and BBB are investment-grade bonds. According to Moody's Aaa to Baa3 are the investment grade bonds. The bonds rated below these grades are high-yielding yet riskier (called junk or non-investment bonds).

Classification with respect to the maturity

Money market securities: Securities with an original maturity of one year or less are called money market securities. U.S. Treasury bills, commercial papers issued by corporations, are some examples of money market fixed-income securities.

Capital market securities: Securities with an original maturity of more than one year are called capital market securities. Fixed deposits and debentures are called capital market securities.

Classification with respect to coupon structure

Bonds are classified as fixed-rate and floating-rate according to their coupon structure. Fixed-rate bonds pay a certain amount periodically, while floating-rate bonds change the coupon rate according to the market rate of interest. Floating-rate bonds provide a hedge against rising interest rates because their coupon payments adjust upward. Conversely, fixed-rate bonds outperform when interest rates fall, as their fixed coupon becomes more attractive. The 'better' instrument depends on the interest rate outlook and the risk tolerance of the investor/issuer.

Geography

Bonds can also be classified with respect to the issuance and trading geography. We have discussed it in very detail previously, as domestic, global, and Eurobonds.

Taxability

Some bonds are tax-exempt (government and government-related bonds are usually tax-exempt), while others are taxed (as income tax and capital gain tax).

Interbank offered rates as reference rates in floating-rate debt

Floating rate debt is often expressed as a reference to the interbank offered rate plus a spread or margin. This margin or spread depends on the credibility of the issuer. **Historically, LIBOR (London Interbank Offered Rate) was the most widely used reference rate.** It has now been largely replaced by new, more robust risk-free rates (RFRs) such as the **Secured Overnight Financing Rate (SOFR)** in the US and the **Sterling Overnight Index Average (SONIA)** in the UK.

The LIBOR or any other interbank offered rate, like Euribor, must match the frequency and maturity of the bond. For example, for a bond with a monthly coupon rate, 30-day LIBOR can be used.

Mechanisms for issuing bonds in primary markets

When the bonds are issued for the first time, they are issued in the primary market. The first issuance can be to the general public (public offering or initial public offering) or to selective investors, called a private placement. When bonds are initially sold, they are subsequently traded in the secondary market.

Public offering is normally done through investment banks.

The investment banks can perform any of the following functions to assist sale of newly issued bonds.

Underwriting: Through underwriting services, the investment banks purchase all the bonds from the issuing entity and then resell them to the public or selected investors. A small number of bonds can be sold by a single bank, but if the quantity of bonds is very large, they are sold through a syndicate of investment banks. The lead underwriter invites other banks to perform these duties. Syndicate (or single bank in case of a small offering) adjusts the price at which the bond would be sold.

Best effort offering: Through best effort offering, the investment banks sell on a commission basis. They earn commission on the number of bonds sold, and the remaining will be returned to the issuers.

Sometimes bonds are issued before a public offering to check the demand for that bond. This is referred to as the _grey market._ Normally, government and government-related bonds, like U.S. Treasury bills, sold through auction are sold through a best effort offering.

Shelf Registration: Through self-registration, bonds are registered with the security regulators in aggregate value. Then the bonds are issued over time whenever the issuer needs funds. Shelf registration is normally allowed for sound and larger companies. These issues can be sold through a public offering or only to selective, qualified investors.

Secondary markets for bonds

When existing bonds (previously issued bonds) are traded, that is called the secondary market. The secondary market can be divided into two types: an organized exchange and the over-the-counter market.

Organized exchange: This is the market where buyers and sellers trade securities with each other, and the price is set through demand and supply. These buyers and sellers can be from anywhere in the world, but they must follow the exchange rules. The exchange market provides higher liquidity. These bonds are cleared through the clearing system. The settlement can be done on the day of trading, T+1, T+2, or T+3. T+1 means settlement within the trade day plus one day. The settlement can take even more than three days in some cases.

Over-the-counter market: In this market, the trade is being done between parties without the supervision of an exchange. This is also called off-exchange trading. In the over-the-counter market, there is less liquidity.

Fixed-income securities issued by sovereign governments

Bonds issued by the national governments for fiscal reasons are called sovereign bonds. These bonds are backed by taxing power and the ability to print new money. That's why these bonds are considered to have the lowest default risk and are typically used as the benchmark 'risk-free' asset in their local currency, though sovereign defaults have occurred.

These bonds can be denominated in local or other currencies. Bonds denominated in local currency are considered higher credit-rated. This is because the government cannot print foreign currency, and taxes are collected in local currency, and its value in foreign currency depends on the exchange rate. US T-bills are a good example of a sovereign bond, and these T-bills are used as a benchmark for other bonds.

Sovereign bonds can be of fixed, floating, or inflation-indexed bonds.

Fixed income securities issued by non-sovereign governments, quasigovernment entities, and supranational agencies

Bonds issued by states, provinces, cities, and regions, and by entities created by states or provinces to fund hospitals, dams, etc., are called non-sovereign government bonds. These bonds are not backed by the national government but by the cash flows from specific projects for which bonds are issued (or can be backed by the cash flows from other projects). These bonds typically trade at a **higher yield than sovereign bonds** due to their lower credit rating and liquidity, though many are still investment-grade. These bonds have a higher credit rating than other bonds but lower than the sovereign bonds.

Quasi-government or agency bonds: Bonds issued by a specially created govt. agencies are quasi-government bonds. These bonds are issued for specific purpose. The national government usually does not back these bonds, but still, these bonds are of a high credit rating because the default risk is extremely low. Yield on these bonds is also high. In the USA, the Federal National Mortgage Association is a government-created agency, and its bonds are quasi-government bonds.

Supranational bonds: Bonds issued by supranational agencies like the World Bank and the IMF are supranational bonds. These agencies are also called multilateral agencies. The credit rating of these bonds is also very high.

Debt from banks

A loan from a single bank (also called a bilateral loan) or a syndicate of banks is the primary source of funds for debt financing. The interest rate on these loans is usually LIBOR-related. Loans originated by a bank can be sold and pooled together by a Special Purpose Entity (SPE) to create a new security called a **securitized bond** or **asset-backed security (ABS)**.

Commercial paper

Sound organizations can issue commercial papers for their short-term funding needs (i.e., working capital) and bridge financing. Bridge financing means commercial papers can fulfill funding needs before the long-term debt securities are issued. Interest rate on commercial papers is very low in comparison to typical bank loans. These papers yield more than sovereign bonds as credit risk is higher as they are issued unsecured. Normally, commercial papers are issued with a maturity of one day to 90 days.

In the USA, commercial papers are issued with a maturity of 270 days or less. This is because when a debt security's maturity goes beyond 270 days, it needs to be registered with SEC and would involve extra cost.

Eurocommercial papers can be issued internationally in any currency with a maturity of less than one year.

Rollover: Usually, the commercial papers are reissued at maturity, called rollover. Sometimes companies cannot reissue and sell new commercial papers because of changes in credit rating or changes in business circumstances. This is called rollover risk. To have a good credit rating, corporations must keep a backup line of credit with banks.

Corporate bonds

Corporations issue bonds with different maturities and coupon structures, which we have discussed before. Bonds with maturity of up to five years are called short-term bonds, with maturity between 5 and

12 years are called medium-term, while maturity of more than 12 years is called long-term bonds.

Medium-term notes

Medium-term notes (MTNs) can be issued by corporations with a maturity of 9 months to 100 years. One should not confuse the name with maturity. These are sold with the help of an agent/dealer to the investor. The investor can choose to buy MTNs of different maturities. The issuing company needs to register with the SEC only once and then can issue MTNs of any maturity at any time. This allows the issuer to tailor its funding requirements. Yield on MTNs is higher than commercial papers. These can be issued with fixed or changing coupon rates (LIBOR-based or index-based).

Structured financial instruments

Structured financing instruments are complex debt instruments that change the risk on the underlying debt. These instruments are usually made by combining debt instruments and derivatives. These instruments are offered to the big companies with complex financing needs, and a mere loan cannot fulfill that requirement. Here are some structured financing instruments.

1. **Asset-backed securities (ABS):** When bonds (or other securities) are issued and their payments are made out of a pool of small or immovable (or a pool of underlying financial assets, such as loans, leases, or receivables) and illiquid assets are called asset-backed securities. The pool that backs these securities is called collateral. These ABS are generally made out of securitized assets like loans, receivables and mortgages. In mortgage-backed securities, the security is backed by only mortgages, while ABS are backed by other debt instruments.

2. **Collateralized debt obligations:** These are instruments backed by one or many debt obligations, like bonds.

3. **Hybrid securities:** These securities are issued as a combination of bond and equity elements.

4. **Credit Linked Note (CLN):** These are securities with an embedded option of a credit swap. It means the issuer can shift a specific credit risk to credit investors. These can be of fixed or floating rates.

Retail market: Deposits by the customers in the banks (retail deposits) are the basic sources of funding for banks. With checking accounts (demand deposits), banks don't have to pay any interest payments, and these funds are immediately available for the bank's funding needs. With savings accounts, banks have to pay some interest, but clients cannot withdraw them immediately.

Certificates of deposits (CDs): Banks also offer certificates of deposits, for which the clients cannot withdraw the money before a maturity date; if they do so, they will have to pay a significant penalty. CDs are also a good source of funding for the banks. The interest rate is higher in CDs.

Negotiable certificates of deposits: These are the short-term instruments issued by banks with a maturity ranging from 2 weeks to 1 year. These certificates can be sold at a discount, or they can give regular interest payments. The minimum face value must be $100000. Subsequently, these certificates are traded in the secondary market.

Interbank market: The banks can get funds from other banks at the interbank rate, usually at the LIBOR rate. These funds can fulfill the short-term needs of the banks. These are the unsecured loans given by one bank to another with a maturity of one day (overnight) to one year.

Central bank funds market: In the US, this is called the FED fund market. The banks operating under the central bank are required to deposit a certain amount with the central bank. Sometimes, some banks have excessive funds (from this reserve requirement) and can lend them to other banks at the central bank rate. These loans can mature from one day to one year. The interest rate depends on the central bank's monetary policy and open market operations.

Repurchase agreements (repos)

A repurchase agreement, or REPO, is an agreement in which one party sells a security to another party with the agreement to buy it back at a specific (higher) price at a later date. The difference between the selling and buying back price is the interest payment by the initial seller (borrower) of the security. The security serves as collateral, and the interest rate is called the repo rate. This repo rate is normally less than a bank loan. If this agreement is for one day, it is called an overnight repo, and if it is for more than one day, it is called a term repo.

Repo margin or haircut: The market value of that contract (bond) might be different from the amount of the loan. The percentage difference between the market value and the amount of the loan is called the repo margin or haircut. For example, a security with a market value of $105 used as collateral for a $100 loan has a haircut of approximately 4.76%. A haircut protects the lender from a decrease in the value of the underlying security.

Factors affecting repo rate and haircut:

The lender of funds is the most vulnerable party in a repo agreement, regardless of collateral. So the repo rate and haircut depend on the following factors.

1. The more the maturity, the higher the repo rate and haircut, and vice versa.
2. The higher the credibility of the borrower and the quality of security, the lower the repo rate and haircut.
3. When collateral is delivered to the lender, the repo rate and haircut would be lower.
4. When the market interest rate is higher, the repo rate and haircut would be higher.
5. If the collateral has higher demand in the market, the repo rate and haircut would be lower.
6.

A reverse repo agreement is an agreement in which the lender of funds sells the security (opposite of buying the collateral as in a normal repo).

Chapter 3: FIXED INCOME VALUATION

The value of a bond is the present value of all future coupon and principal payments. This present value is calculated using the market discount rate, also called yield to maturity or redemption yield.

Value of bond with annual coupon payment:

For example, a 4-year bond with a face value of $100, a coupon rate is 5% annually, and a market discount rate is 5% calculate the present value of the bond or simply the value of the bond.

$$\text{Value of bond} = \frac{5}{1.05^1} + \frac{5}{1.05^2} + \frac{5}{1.05^3} + \frac{105}{1.05^4} = 100$$

The present value of this bond is $100. Note that when the coupon rate and discount rate are the same, the present value of all future payments is equal to the par value.

For calculator input values are as follows;

N (number of years) =4, PMT (coupon payment) =5, FV=100, 1/Y (discount rate) =5.

If the discount rate is more than the coupon rate, the bond would be sold at a discount. For example, if the discount rate is 10% the value of the same bond would be

Value of bond $= \frac{5}{1.1^1} + \frac{5}{1.1^2} + \frac{5}{1.1^3} + \frac{105}{1.1^4} = 84.15$ this is called discounted bond

So when the bond yield increases, the present value and market value of the bond decrease.

And when the market yield (discount rate) decreases, the present value (or the market value) of the bond increases, called a premium bond.

Value of bond with semi-annual coupon payment: Consider the same bond with a 10% annual coupon rate semi-annually. The discount rate is also 10%. We need to convert a 10% annual coupon rate into a semi-annual as 10/2=5% of the face value. Now the discounting periods are doubled (twice every year), so we have 4x2 = 8 periods of payment. The discount rate would also be divided by 2 as 10/2=5%.

Value of bond $= \dfrac{5}{1.05^1} + \dfrac{5}{1.05^2} + \dfrac{5}{1.05^3} + \dfrac{5}{1.05^4} + \dfrac{5}{1.05^5} + \dfrac{5}{1.05^6} + \dfrac{5}{1.05^7} +$

$\dfrac{105}{1.05^8} = 100$

If the price of the bond, the number of years, and the coupon rates are given, we can also calculate the yield to maturity. The YTM would be the rate that makes the present value of future cash flow equal to the price of the bond.

Relationships among a bond's price, coupon rate, maturity, and market discount rate (yield-to-maturity).

- As we have discussed previously, the discount rate (yield to maturity) is inversely related to the market value of the bond. When the discount rate increases (decreases), the price of the bond decreases (increases). When the discount rate (YTM) and the coupon rate are equal, the bond is at par. When YTM is greater than the coupon rate, the bond is at a discount, and when YTM is less than the coupon rate, the bond is at a premium.

- When YTM increases, the percentage decrease in value of the bond is smaller than the increase in the bond's value as YTM decreases by the same amount. So the price-to-yield relationship is convex.

- The bond with a lower coupon rate is more sensitive to a change in YTM than a bond with a higher coupon rate.
- The bond with a higher maturity term is more sensitive to changes in YTM than a bond with a lower maturity. This is because when a bond's maturity is longer, it will be discounted more times.

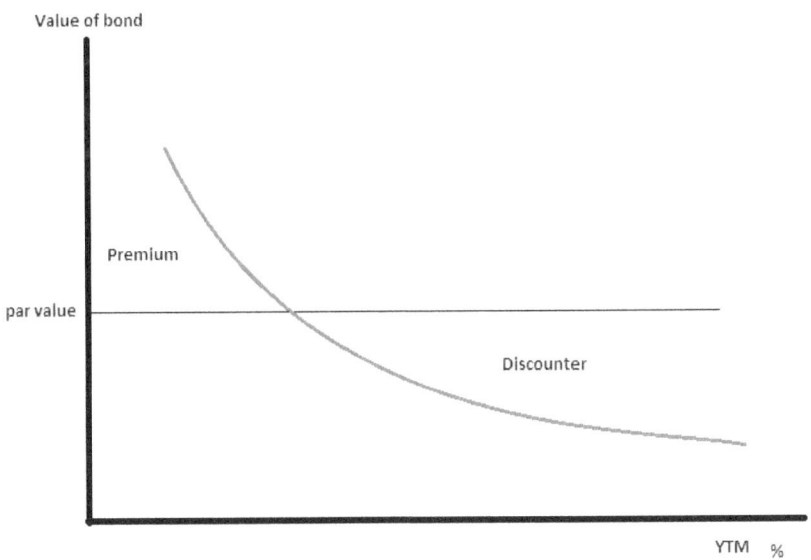

Before maturity, the bond can be traded at par, at a discount, or at a premium. Regardless of the current value of the bond, the price will converge to the par as the maturity approaches. This convergence is called a constant-yield price trajectory.

Spot rates

Spot rates are the yield to maturity (discount rate) on zero-coupon bonds maturing at each cash flow date. Yield to maturity is calculated as the discount rate is the same for every bond. But actually, the discount rate depends on the timing of each cash flow, that is why the spot rate is more relevant for discounting a bond. This discount rate on zero-coupon bonds is also called zero-coupon rates or zero rates. To calculate the bond's price using the spot rate, we discount each cash flow by its own spot rate and sum all the results as follows;

$$\text{Value of bond} = \frac{CF1}{1+S1^1} + \frac{CF2}{(1+S2)^2} + \frac{CF3}{(1.+3)^3} + \frac{CF4}{(1+S4)^4} + \frac{CF5}{1+S5} \cdots \cdots \frac{CFn}{(1+S)^n}$$

CF1 = first cash flow on that bond

CF2 = second cash flow on that bond

CFn= Final cash flow of bond. It consists of a coupon plus the principal amount.

S1 = the spot rate at the time of first cash flow

S2 = spot rate at time of second cash flow

Sn= spot rate at time of maturity.

For example, we have a 3-year bond with an FV of $100 and a coupon rate is 5%. Spot rates are

1-year spot rate=2%

2-year spot rate =4%

5-year spot rate 5%.

Then value of bond $= \frac{5}{1.02^1} + \frac{5}{(1.04)^2} + \frac{105}{(1.05)^3} = 100.22$

As the price of the bond is greater than its FV, the YTM would be less than its coupon rate.

By using a calculator, we can calculate YTM by inputting the following data.

N=3, PMT=5, FV=100, PV= 100.22 calculate 1/y

The bond price using the spot rate is also called the no-arbitrage price. So when the price is different from 100.22, in our case, there would be a profitable opportunity.

So far, we have calculated the bond's price on the coupon payment date. The price of a bond differs between coupon payments. This price has two components: the flat price (PV flat) and accrued interest (AI). The full price (PV full) is the sum of AI and the flat price. This full price is also called the dirty price. PV flat + AI = PV full

The flat value can be calculated on a specific date is simply the present value of remaining coupons and principal amount.

Accrued interest can be calculated as

$AI = (t/T) \times PMT$

T is the number of days passed from the last coupon payment.

T = Total number of days between two payments.

The method of estimation of the price of a bond that is not being actively traded (or not being traded) is called matrix pricing. This estimation is used to calculate the price and YTM of infrequently traded bonds. We use the prices of the other most actively traded bonds with similar credit quality, maturity date, and coupon rate in estimation.

For example, we have illiquid bond A with a coupon rate of 5% and a maturity of 3 years.

We also found two related bonds with an active market as follows;

Bond Y with 4years of maturity and a coupon rate of 5.5% at a price of 102.

Bond Z with 2 years of maturity and a coupon rate of 4.5% at a price of 101.

The YTM on bond Y can be calculated as

With bond Y, we have

N=4, PV=-102, PMT=5.5, FV=100, calculate 1/y

With bond Z, we have

N=2, PV=-101, PMT=4.5, FV=100, calculate 1/y

When we have YTM on these two bonds, we can take the average of the YTMs of the two bonds and use it as the estimated YTM on our bond A. for instance, We can **interpolate** between the YTMs of the two bonds based on maturity to estimate the YTM for our 3-year bond. For example, if the 2-year YTM is 2% and the 4-year YTM is 4%, the estimated 3-year YTM might be 3%. From here, we can calculate the price of our bond using this average YTM.

Matrix pricing can also be used in the underwriting process to get an estimation of YTM and spread over a benchmark (mostly a similar government bond).

Annual yield and varying compounding periods in a year

Annual yield = {1+(i/n)}^n)-1

"n" is the number of compounding annually.

"i" is a nominal yield

For example, an annual paying 4% YTM bond has an annual yield (also called effective yield) of 4%.

Annual yield = [{1+(i/n)}^2]-1 = [{1+ (0.004/1)}^1] − 1 =4 %.

Semiannual bond with 4% nominal yield has annual yield of ((1+0.04/2) ^2} − 1 = 4.04%.

In the same way, we can calculate annual yields for quarterly, monthly, or any periodicity.

Yield measures for fixed-rate bonds and floating-rate notes

YTM is the rate of discount that equalizes the present value of all future cash flows of a bond to its price.

Yield Measures for Fixed-rate bonds

Yield to maturity: The YTM depends on the number of coupon payments in a year.

Effective yield: Effective yield is a measure of return assuming that the amount received (coupon payment) is reinvested at the same interest rate.

Effective yield = $\{1+(YTM/n)\}^{\wedge}n)-1$

"n" is the number of compounding annually.

For example, an annual paying 4% YTM bond has an effective yield of 4%. Semiannual bond with 4% annual YTM has a yield of $4/2 = 2\%$ every six months, and the effective yield is $((1+0.04/2)^{\wedge}2 -1 =$ 4.04%.

Effective yield is used to convert the YTM to a comparable mode.

Current yield: It is calculated by dividing the annual coupon payments and bond's price

$$\text{Current yield} = \frac{\text{Annual coupon payment}}{\text{Current market price of bond}}$$

This measure is very simple and does not account the capital gain/loss, and does not give us any other information.

Street conversion: Street conversion assumes that the coupon payments are made on the actual date (on Saturdays and Sundays if stated so).

True yield: True yield is calculated by taking the dates on which the coupon payments are made. If the stated payment date is on a weekend, they are actually paid on the next working day. So the true yields are slightly lower than the street conversion.

Yield to worst: This measure is used to calculate yield in the worst-case scenario to help the investor manage risk. This is the lowest potential yield that an investor would receive without the issuer actually defaulting.

Yield to call: It is calculated for each call date of a security.

Yields on Floating Rate Notes (FRNs)

The return on floating rate notes is adjusted periodically according to the reference (Usually LIBOR) plus/minus a margin. Due to the flexibility of interest rate (rate of return), the price of FRNs is generally more stable. This margin depends on the credit risk of the issuer. The rate quoted on FRNs is called *the quoted margin, and the margin to make its present value equal to its par value is called the* *required margin*. If the credit risk of the issuer increases (decreases) over the term of the FRN, the quoted margin would be lower (higher) than the required margin, and the FRN will be sold at a discount (premium). With no change in credit risk, these two would be equal at each reset point, and the price would be at par.

The rule for calculation is the same here. At each reset date, the current reference rate is used to calculate future cash flow and discount it at the required rate.

Yield measures for fixed money market instruments

Yields for Money Market Instruments

The yield on money market instruments is calculated as a discount from face value or an add-on yield using 360 or 365 days. US T-bills are quoted as an annual discount rate using 360 days. The CDs are quoted with an add-on rate using 365 days. So the difference between the discount rate and the add-on rate is only the total days in the calculation.

Formulae

$$\text{Discount rate} = \frac{\textit{days in a year}}{\textit{number of days in maturity of intrument}} * \frac{FV - PV}{PV}$$

$$\text{ADD on rate} = \frac{\textit{days in a year}}{\textit{number of days in maturity of intrument}} * \frac{FV - PV}{PV}$$

Spot curve, yield curve on coupon bonds, par curve, and forward curve

Spot rate curve: YTM on zero-coupon bonds is called the spot rate. The curve representing this relationship between YTM on a zero-coupon bond and the maturity of the bond is called the spot rate curve, strip curve, or zero curve.

U.S. Treasury bonds are considered zero-coupon bonds. The higher the maturity, the higher the YTM is.

Yield curve for coupon bonds: The Curve shows the relationship between yield and maturity of coupon bonds. Again, higher maturities have higher yield.

Par bond yield curve: Also called par curve. It is not constructed from the actual cash payments but from the spot rate curve. A par yield is the yield for which a bond is priced at par. Consider a 4-year annual coupon bond, and spot rates are as follows;

1-year spot rate is $S1=2\%$

2-year spot rate is $S2=1.8\%$

3-year spot rate is $S3=2.1\%$

4-year spot rate is $S4=2.2\%$

We can calculate the par bond yield as

$$\frac{PMT}{(1+S1)^1} + \frac{PMT}{(1+S2)^2} + \frac{PMT}{(1+S3)^3} + \frac{100+PMT}{(1+S4)^4}$$

$$\frac{PMT}{(1+0.02)^1} + \frac{PMT}{(1+0.018)^2} + \frac{PMT}{(1+0.021)^3} + \frac{100+PMT}{(1+0.022)^4}$$

Solving for PMT, we will have the par bond yield.

Forward rates: The interest rate for contracts (in our case, bonds or other debt instruments) for future payments is the forward rate. In other words, the rate of interest on a loan (or any other debt) with similar maturity on a future date is called the forward rate. A curve shows these rates with different maturities, which is a forward rate curve.

Forward rates-spot rates, and the price of a bond using forward rates

The forward rate is the interest rate on a loan beginning at some future date. Spot rate is the interest rate on a loan beginning immediately. Forward rate for 1y2y means the forward rate from one year from now for a two-year loan. First notion (1y) states the future date, and the second notion (2y) states the term of the loan.

Relationship between forward rates and spot rates

Logically, borrowing for 4 years at a 4-year spot rate and borrowing for one year for 4 consecutive years must be at the same cost. This logic can be expressed in the following equation.

$$(1 + S4)^4 = (1 + S1)(1 + 1y1y)(1 + 2y1y)(1 + 3y1y)$$

The left-hand side shows the four spot rates for 4 consecutive years, while the right-hand side shows forward rates. First term (1+S1) states that in the first year, it is the current rate that would be used. Ok, solve the previous equation for S4

$$S4 = \{(1 + S1)(1 + 1y1y)(1 + 2y1y)(1 + 3y1y)\}^{1/4} - 1$$

This term on the right-hand side is simply the geometric mean of three terms.

This very same relationship can be used to calculate the forward rate with a given spot rate.

Calculation of the bond's value using forward rates:

This is also a very simple calculation. Just discount every cash payment of the bond by the forward rate for each period.

Bond value using forward rate

$$= \frac{PMT1}{1 + S1} + \frac{PMT2}{(1 + S1)(1 + 1y1y)}$$

$$+ \frac{PMT3}{(1 + S1)(1 + 1y1y)(1 + 2y1y)} \cdots \frac{PMTn}{(1 + S1)(1 + 1y1y)((1 + ny1y)}$$

Yield spread: The Difference between the yields of two different bonds is called the yield spread.

This spread is usually calculated with respect to a benchmark called the _benchmark spread._ For example, a 2-year corporate bond yield is 5% and a 2-year government bond yield is 3%. The yield spread of the corporate bond is 5-3= 2%. This yield spread is usually calculated in basis points. We know that 1% is equal to 100 basis points. So yield spread in our case is 200 basis points. Yield spread with respect to government security is also called _G-spread_.

The yield spread must be calculated by comparing two securities of the same maturity. Yield spread can also change during the life of the bond. For example, when a 4-year bond is issued, it is compared with a 5-year security, and after 1 year passes, its spread can be compared with a security with a maturity of 4 years.

Yield spread can also be calculated with respect to a swap (with the same currency). This is known as an *interpolated spread (I-spread).*

For analysis, if the yield on a specific security rises but the spread remains the same, it means overall yields have risen due to economic growth (or any other macroeconomic variable). On the other hand, if the spread has risen, the credit risk of the issuer may be increased.

Z-spread or zero volatility spread: The yield on bonds increases with maturity. The simple spread will increase as the maturity of the bond increases. So the simple yield spreads (I-spread and G-spread) have this disadvantage because they show higher yield with higher maturity.

To eliminate this problem, we have Z-spread. To calculate Z-spread, we have to add some appropriate amount to the benchmark so that the new benchmark yield equals the price of the bond to its market value. This is how we calculate z-spread.

$$\text{Market price of bond} = \frac{\text{coupon PMT}}{\text{benchmark}+Z} + \frac{\text{coupon PMT}}{\text{benchmark}+Z} + \frac{\text{coupon PMT}}{\text{benchmark}+Z} \cdots$$

$$\frac{\text{coupon PMTn}}{\text{benchmark}+Z}$$

If we are given the market price, the coupon payment, and the benchmark, we can calculate the Z-spread with the help of this equation on a trial-and-error basis. Remember that Z must be constant across all periods.

The Z-spread tends to be higher (lower) with more (less) credit risk.

Option-adjusted spread: The option-adjusted spread is calculated for the bonds with options of call or put. A simple spread or z-spread cannot accurately calculate the yield on a callable/puttable bond.

We know that the price of a callable bond is less than equivalent non-callable bond. So we calculate the option-adjusted spread by removing the option on that bond.

Option embedded spread = Z-spread – option value

CHAPTER 4: INTRODUCTION TO ASSET-BACKED SECURITIES

Securitization and its benefits

Securitization: Securitization is a process in which debt instruments like receivables, loans, mortgages, etc., are purchased by an entity (called SPE or special purpose entity, special purpose vehicle, or special purpose company) which then issues securities backed by those debts. The cash flows on newly issued securities are backed by the cash flow from those debt assets (instruments).

Benefits

- The firm selling its financial debt can immediately raise capital to use.
- The backed illiquid financial assets (debts) are now liquid with new security. This new security can be traded in the secondary market.
- The credit risk of the firm selling these assets is transferred to new entity.

- A financial company or bank is able to lend more with securitization. Without securitization, the bank's lending was limited to traditional assets.

- The investors seeking to invest in debt have more options according to their risk tolerance and return.

- Securitization also increases the diversification, which reduces risk.

Securitization process

Consider L-Corporation, which provides autos on installment to its customers. It means the corporation is giving loans to its customers and gets installment payments on the loans periodically. Suppose it has sold worth $100000 autos to its customers. This $100000 is a debt asset for an L-corporation. The corporation then establishes an SPE and sells these loans of $100000 to it. The SPE is a separate entity from an L-corporation. The SPE issues a new security backed by this $100000 and sells it to the investors. The newly issued security can be in different classes according to face value, interest rates, payment priorities, and claims on assets in case of default. These classes are called the *waterfall structure*. Investors have a claim on the SPE's assets, but no claim against L-Corporation. The L-corporation continues to receive the installments (principal and interest). The L-corporation is the issuer and lender. The issuer and lender can be the same or different. So, we have the following parties with their roles;

Customers: The customers buy autos from L-corporation and pay the amount in installments.

Seller and servicer: The L-Corporation is the seller of autos. It is also the lender who provides loans to these customers but transfers the debt to SPE and receives $100000 from SPE (which is ultimately from investors).

SPE: The organization is specially designed for securitization. It will issue debt securities (asset-backed securities, ABS) to investors, get the amount, and pay to the Issuer and lender.

Investors: The investors will receive the periodic interest payment and principal at maturity.

Typical structures of securitizations

Newly issued security in securitization can be of a single class or multiple classes. In a single class, all securities are of the same credit risk, and holders of such securities have equal claims on assets. These different classes of ABS are called tranches. In tranche, different classes of ABS holders have different claims on cash flows, and the risk is redistributed. Some have more risk than others. Remember, total credit risk remains the same, only redistributed.

Credit tranching/Senior-subordinate structure: Tranching according to credit risk is called credit tranching. In this structure, more than one ABS class is issued. One is the senior class, the other is the subordinate class A, the Subordinate class B, and so on. If an ABS is issued with three classes mentioned above as senior, subordinate A, and subordinate B, then the subordinate B is of the highest risk and also with the highest return. If the creditor defaults, the subordinate B class will lose its money up to a limit. If the loss goes beyond that limit, the exceeding loss of principal amount has to be borne by Subordinate B up to their limit. If that limit also crosses, then the senior class will bear that loss. The senior class is the least risky (highest in credit rating), so they earn the lowest yield.

As each class receives overflow from its senior class in case of liquidation, this structure is also called the _waterfall structure_.

Time tranching: When ABS are issued with different maturities it is called time tranching.

Types and characteristics of securitized residential mortgage loans

Residential mortgage: A Residential mortgage is a loan that uses real estate as collateral. If the borrower defaults, the lender has the right to resell the collateral to recover funds. This process of taking possession of collateral and reselling is called foreclosure.

The amount of the loan is less than the value of the property used as collateral. The ratio of loan to the value of the property is called the loan-to-value ratio. The lower the LTV, the more the lender is protected.

Two types of mortgage loans usually exist: the prime loan and the subprime loan. The prime loan is given to customers with a high credit rating and typically features a **lower** Loan-to-Value (LTV) ratio. A **subprime loan** is given to customers with lower credit quality and often has a **higher** LTV ratio, meaning the borrower has less equity in the property, or when the collateral used is already being used in another loan (a lower claim of the lender on the property).

The nature of mortgages differs in different countries. The mortgages can be differentiated with respect to their characteristics like maturity, interest rate determination, amortization schedule, prepayment options and penalties, and foreclosure.

Maturity: This is the duration of the loan until complete repayment. The term of a mortgage loan is usually long. In the US, the usual term of a mortgage falls between 15 and 30 years. In Europe, the term can be from 20 to 40 years.

Interest rate determination:

Fixed rate mortgage: This is a mortgage in which the interest rate will remain the same during the lifetime of the loan.

Variable rate mortgage: In this mortgage, the interest rate is adjusted periodically according to the prevailing rate in the market or according to some reference, like LIBOR. Usually, the variable rate mortgage interest rate is given as some spread over LIBOR.

Hybrid mortgage: A mortgage can be with a fixed interest rate in its initial stages, but after some time it can be a variable mortgage. This is called hybrid mortgage.

Negotiable mortgage: If the interest rate in a hybrid mortgage is changed, fixed to a new interest rate, it is called a rollover or renegotiable mortgage.

Convertible mortgage: If, after some time, the mortgage is converted from a fixed rate to a variable rate (or vice versa) for the rest of its life, with the consent of the borrower, it is called a convertible mortgage.

Amortization schedule of principal amount:

Fully amortized loan: With a fully amortized mortgage loan, the periodic payment includes some principal and some interest. When the final payment is made there is no interest or principal amount is left. If the payment amount is fixed, initially the payment includes more interest and less principal, which will reverse with the passage of time (in later years, the payment includes less interest and more principal amount.

Partially amortized loan: In this mortgage, the periodic payments include some amount of principal, and the rest is interest. The principal amount is not fully amortized during the term of the loan. At the end of the loan, a lump sum of the principal amount is paid.

Interest-only or balloon loan: With this mortgage, the periodic payments only include the interest, and at the end of the term, the full principal amount is repaid.

Prepayment and penalties:

Prepayments are the partial or full repayment of the principal amount by the borrower before the time. Sometimes the borrower can find another loan with a lower interest rate and prepay the first loan with the second loan. Mostly, the mortgage loan (and other loans too) have a provision of a penalty for early payment. This protects the lender in case of a decrease in interest rate during the term of the loan. The penalty is an excessive amount over the principal amount that the borrower has to pay for early payment.

Foreclosure: In case of default of the borrower, the lender has the right to take possession of the collateral and resell it to generate cash. The value of collateral must be higher than the amount of the loan. If the value of the property substantially decreases, the borrower can voluntarily give the possession to the lender. This is called strategic default. To protect the lender from this, sometimes the mortgages are recourse loans. In recourse loans, the lender has the right on the borrower equal to the amount of the decrease in value of collateral. Recourse loan is common in Europe and is also in use in the USA.

The securities issued from the securitization of mortgages are called residential mortgage-backed securities (RMBS). In the USA, these securities can be divided into three categories.

1. The federal government guaranteed RMBS (agency RMBS). These are considered to have the highest credibility.
2. RMBS guaranteed by government-sponsored enterprises (like Fannie Mae and Freddie Mac). These are also considered agency RMBS. Less credibility than the first one, but still good credibility.
3. RMBS issued by private entities (non-agency RMBS). Less credible than the above two.

Mortgage pass-through securities: When one or more mortgage holders sell share or participation certificates to the pool. The cash flow from the collateral pool passes through to the security holders as coupon and principal payments. All agency RMBS are pass-through securities. The mortgages are of different maturities, so the weighted average maturities (WAM) and weighted average coupon rate (WAC) are applied to pass-through cash flows.

Prepayment risk of mortgage-backed securities

There are two types of risks associated with MBS: a decline in interest rate and a rise in interest rate. When the interest rate declines, the clients buy other lower-interest loans and pay back the first mortgage before time (prepayments). In this scenario, the issuer of the mortgage receives fewer revenues as the payments of interest rates fall and the mortgage maturity reduces. (Also called contraction risk as the interest rate falls).

Agency MBS are exposed to a significant prepayment risk as they have no penalty provision for early payment.

Single monthly mortality rate (SMM) is the one way to calculate contraction risk on a monthly basis.

$$SMM = \frac{Prepayments\ for\ the\ month}{Mb-scheduled\ principal\ repayment\ for\ the\ month}$$

Mb is *Begining outstanding mortgage balance*

The annualized SMM is called the conditional prepayment rate (CPR)

$CPR = (1+SMM) \wedge (12) - 1$

A lower SMM and CPR are desirable.

When the interest rate rises, the prepayments are less than expected. Rising interest rate is the opportunity cost of the issuer of the mortgage (also called extension risk as the interest rate rises).

Commercial mortgage-backed securities

Commercial mortgage-backed securities (CMBS) are the securities backed by a pool of commercial mortgages. Commercial mortgages are on income-producing properties (real estate). These real estates can be multi-family apartments, warehouses, office buildings, shopping centers, etc. The CMBS are repaid by investors of these properties, while the residential MBS are repaid by the homeowners.

Credit risk: CMBS are typically structured as **non-recourse** loans. This means the lender's claim is limited only to the commercial property serving as collateral, and they cannot seek repayment from the borrower's other assets. This is why the analysis focuses solely on the property's income and value (not on the borrower of the loan). Two ratios are considered to calculate the credit risk of CMBS: the debt-service coverage ratio (debt coverage ratio) and the loan-to-value ratio.

Debt-service coverage ratio$= \dfrac{\textit{Net operating income}}{\textit{Debt service}}$

Net operating income = income from property – property taxes

Debt service = Principal repayments and interest payments

A higher ratio shows less risk as income is being generated sufficiently from the property.

$$\text{Loan to value ratio} = \frac{Current\ mortgage\ amount}{current\ appraised\ value\ of\ property}$$

Appraised value of the property is the value that is determined by the lender (not by the market). Usually, it is the value that will be received when the property is sold immediately.

The lower this ratio is, the more desirable it is for the lender. This ratio shows how many times the current amount of the mortgage can be paid with the property value.

Structure

Credit rating agencies assess the credit risk of CMBS. These CMBS are structured in tranches, and the lowest priority tranche is usually excluded in credit risk calculation.

CMBS usually have a call provision which protects investors against prepayments. There are two types of call protection

Loan-level call protection and CMBS structure call protection.

Loan level call protection: This call protection can be in any one of four ways.

Prepayment lockout: This provision restricts the borrower from prepayment for a specific period.

Defeasance: In this, the borrower puts some funds or a portfolio of the lowest risk (or high credibility) to repay the principal and or interest amount.

Prepayment penalty point: Points are fixed as a penalty for early payments. Each point represents 1% of principal prepayment.

Yield maintenance charges: In this provision, the charges are paid equivalent to the lender's loss of interest rate. This makes the borrower and lender indifferent to whether to pay early or not.

All these penalties are distributed among investors according to the structure of CMBS.

CMBS structure call protection:

In this, the CMBS is divided into different tranches (higher priority and lower priority), and different call provisions are applied to different tranches.

Mostly, the CMBS are structured in a way that the borrower has to pay a huge amount at the end of the loan term. This is called a *balloon payment*. The risk attached to a balloon payment is called *balloon risk.* If the borrower defaults, the lender is required to extend the period of the loan. This extended period is called the *workout period*. The interest rate is higher in the workout period due to the increased risk of default.

Non-mortgage asset-backed securities

There are some ABS which are not backed by mortgages but by other financial assets like receivables, business loans, credit card receivable loans, and home loans, etc. These are called non-mortgage asset-backed securities.

Auto loan ABS: ABS backed by auto loans is called auto loan ABS. The cash flow components of these ABS are principal repayments, interest payments and prepayments. These ABS have senior/subordinate structures.

Credit card receivable-backed ABS: Securities created from the credit card receivables. The cash flow components of these ABS include finance charges, principal, and annual charges. These are non-amortizing loans, as the balances on credit cards are revolving. The investors of these ABS are paid periodically but not during the lockout period (if any). Interest rate on credit card ABS can be fixed or floating. Sometimes, in order to maintain credit quality, early (rapid) amortization is required.

A collateralized debt obligation (CDO) is a security backed by debt obligations like corporate and other bonds. CDO is usually issued by SPE and does not rely on interest payment like ABS. The manager of CDOs actively trades securities to generate promised cash flows to investors. CDOs backed by other CMBS, RMBS, ABS, and other CDOs are called structured CDOs. CDOs backed by SWAPS are called synthetic CDOs.

Structure of CDO

SPE issues the CDOs, and the manager of the CDO buys and sells the debt obligations from the CDO pool and generates cash flows. The funds are created by issuing CDOs to investors. These CDOs are also issued in senior/subordinate classes.

Risks: Like other securities, there is a risk of a fall in interest rate and default risk. All risks are ultimately borne by the CDO investors.

CHAPTER 4: FIXED INCOME RISK AND RETURN

Sources of return from investing in a fixed-rate bond

Assuming all coupon and principal payments are made on time and that coupon payments can be reinvested at the original yield-to-maturity (YTM), the return from a fixed-rate bond comes from four sources:

1. The coupon payments.
2. The repayment of the principal.
3. The interest earned on the reinvestment of coupon payments.
4. A capital gain or loss if the bond is sold before maturity.

If an investor buys a bond and holds it to maturity, and all coupons are reinvested at the original YTM, the investor's annualized rate of return will be equal to the YTM at the time of purchase.

If an investor sells the bond before maturity, the realized rate of return will only equal the original YTM if the bond's yield remains unchanged until the sale date *and* all received coupons were reinvested at that original YTM.

If market rates increase after purchase, the investor can reinvest coupon payments at a higher rate. This results in a realized return greater than the original YTM.

Conversely, if market rates decrease, coupons are reinvested at a lower rate. This results in a realized return **less than** the original YTM."

Macaulay, modified, and effective durations

Macaulay duration is the weighted average term to maturity of a bond's cash flows. It was developed by Frederick Macaulay and serves as a measure of a bond's interest rate sensitivity. Specifically, it represents the weighted average time an investor must hold the bond for the present value of its cash flows to equal the price paid.

$$\text{Macaulay duration} = \sum_{t=1}^{n} \frac{tC}{(1+\text{YTM})^t} + \frac{nV}{(1+\text{YTM})^n} \div \text{MP}$$

t= period in which the coupon is received

n= total number of periods

C=Coupon payments

YTM is the yield to maturity or required yield

V=Maturity value

MP= Market price of bond

While the formula appears complex, its calculation is straightforward: it is the sum of the present values of all cash flows, each weighted by the time until they are received, divided by the bond's current market price.

Consider a 3-year, $100 bond with an annual coupon rate of 10%.

Period	Cash flow	Cash flow x period	Present value of each cash flow
1	10	10	9.09091
2	10	20	16.53
3	110	330	247.93
Total			273.551

Macaulay duration = 273.551/100 = 2.73

Now that the bond has a sensitivity of 2.73. If the interest rate changes by 30 basis points, Macaulay duration would change by 2.73 x 0.0030 = 0.00819 duration.

Modified duration: It shows the percentage change in the price of a bond due to a percentage change in the yield to maturity.

Modified duration = Macaulay duration/ (1+YTM/q)

Where q is the number of times a bond pays in one year. For an annual bond, q is 1, and for a semi-annual bond, q is 2.

Using previous case

Modified duration (ModDur) = 2.73/1.1) = 2.48

2.48 shows that if YTM increases by 1 percent, the price of the bond will fall by 2.48 percent.

Effective duration is used when the previously discussed methods (Macaulay and modified duration) are insufficient. Those methods assume an **option-free security**—one with no embedded call or put options and no prepayment risk. However, these embedded options alter a bond's cash flow pattern, which in turn affects its yield and price sensitivity.

Effective duration accounts for these optionality features by measuring the expected price sensitivity of a bond based on potential changes in the benchmark yield curve. It is calculated by estimating the bond's price change for both a small increase and a small decrease in yield.

$$\text{Effective duration} = \frac{P- - P+}{\{(2*P0)*(Y- - Y+)}$$

P- is the price of bond if yield falls by x basis points.

P+ is the price of bond if yield rises by x basis points.

Po is the initial price of bond.

Y- - Y+ is the changes in yield.

Key rate duration and its uses in measuring the sensitivity of bonds

Traditional duration measures are primarily useful for assessing interest rate risk under the assumption of a parallel shift in the benchmark yield curve. However, when the yield curve changes shape—such as steepening or flattening—these measures become less effective.

Key rate duration (also known as partial duration) addresses this limitation. It measures the sensitivity of a bond's (or portfolio's) price to a change in the benchmark yield at a specific maturity point. For a portfolio, the key rate duration is calculated for each relevant maturity, and the total price impact of a non-parallel shift is the sum of these individual effects.

How a bond's maturity, coupon, and yield level affect its interest rate risk

Maturity and Interest Rate Risk: All else being equal, a bond with a longer maturity is more sensitive to changes in interest rates. This is because cash flows received further in the future are discounted more heavily. Consequently, a bond with a shorter time to maturity has less interest rate risk.

Coupon Rate and Interest Rate Risk: Holding all other factors constant, a bond with higher coupon payments has lower interest rate risk, while a bond with lower coupon payments has higher interest rate risk.

Yield and Interest Rate Risk: The higher a bond's yield, the lower its interest rate risk. Conversely, the lower a bond's yield, the higher its interest rate risk.

Duration of a portfolio and its limitations

There are two primary methods for calculating the duration of a portfolio:

1. **Weighted Average Time Until the Receipt of Cash Flows**
2. **Weighted Average of the Duration of Each Bond**

The first method is theoretically superior but often difficult to implement in practice. The second method is more straightforward to calculate but comes with significant limitations.

1. Weighted Average Time Until the Receipt of Cash Flows

This approach is based on the portfolio's internal rate of return (IRR), or cash flow yield. The calculation is as follows:

$$\text{Total value of portfolio} = \frac{\text{Cash flow1}}{(1+r)^1} + \frac{\text{Cash flow2}}{(1+r)^2} + \ldots\ldots \frac{\text{Cash flow'n}}{(1+r)^n}$$

And calculate for r.

Limitations of the Cash Flow Yield Method:

This approach cannot be applied when future cash flows are uncertain, which is the case for bonds with embedded options (e.g., callable or putable bonds) or floating-rate bonds. Furthermore, interest rate risk is not typically expressed as a spread to a benchmark in this framework. Additionally, a single cash flow yield is not conventionally calculated for an entire bond portfolio. Finally, the method is often impractical to implement due to its complexity.

Weighted Average Duration of Individual Bonds:

This method calculates the portfolio's duration by taking the weighted average of the durations of each constituent bond.

Portfolio duration = W1 D1 + W2 D2 + ... + Wn Dn

W1 is the weight of the first bond, which is calculated as the full price of that bond divided by the total value of the portfolio.

W2 is the weight of the second bond, and so on.

D1 is the duration of the first bond, D2 is the duration of the second bond, and so on.

N is the number of bonds in the portfolio.

Limitations of the Weighted Average Method:

While this method is more practical—as it can be used for bonds with embedded options by employing effective duration—it is generally less accurate than the cash flow yield method. Its primary limitation is the key assumption that the yield change must be parallel across all maturities (i.e., the entire yield curve shifts by the same amount). If the yields of the individual bonds do not change by the same amount, this measure becomes less meaningful.

Money duration of a bond and price value of a basis point (PVBP)

We know that modified duration measures the percentage change in price of a bond due to the percentage change in yield to maturity.

Money duration (in the US called dollar duration) measures the change in bond price in absolute terms (in currency).

Money duration = full price + Annual modified duration

Δ full price $\cong$ – MoneyDur x ΔYield

Money duration is also expressed as money duration per 100 of the bond par value.

Money duration per 100 units of par value = annual modified duration × full bond price per 100 of par value

The **Price Value of a Basis Point (PVBP)**, also known as Dollar Value of a 01 (DV01)**,** is the change in a bond's full price (dirty price) resulting from a one basis point (0.01%) change in its yield to maturity (YTM). It quantifies the dollar amount of interest rate risk for a given position.

PVBP = Δ full price/ Δ YTM

Approximate convexity and effective convexity

While modified duration provides a linear approximation of the relationship between yield changes and bond price changes, the actual relationship is **convex**, not linear. Due to this curvature, the modified duration estimate becomes less accurate for larger yield movements.

Convexity describes the fact that as a bond's yield increases, its price decreases, but **at a decreasing rate**. Conversely, as yield falls, the price increases at an increasing rate. This property benefits the bondholder, as convexity helps to mitigate price declines when yields rise and amplifies price gains when yields fall.

In technical terms, **convexity** is a measure of the curvature in the relationship between a bond's price and its yield. It quantifies the sensitivity of the duration itself to changes in yield.

$$\text{Approximate Convexity} = \frac{\{P(i \text{ decreased}) + P(i \text{ increased}) - 2P0\}}{P0(\Delta YTM)^2}$$

P(i decrease) means the price of the bond when the interest rate falls.

P(i increase) means the price of the bond when the interest rate increases.

P0 is the initial price, which is the face value.

When there are embedded options with the bond, we use effective convexity.

$$\text{Approximate effective convexity} = \frac{\{P(i \text{ decreased}) + P(i \text{ increased}) - 2P0\}}{P0(\Delta curve)^2}$$

Bonds with embedded options have more convexity than option-free similar bonds. Longer maturity bonds, lower coupon rate, and lower YTM are also exposed to more convexity.

Term structure of yield volatility and interest rate risk of a bond

The relationship between a bond's yield volatility and its time to maturity is known as the term structure of interest rates or the term structure of yield volatility.

A bond's price sensitivity to interest rate changes depends primarily on its duration and convexity. For investors, the primary concern is the potential price volatility of the bond.

Contrary to what might be intuitively assumed, a bond with a shorter maturity generally exhibits less price volatility for a given change in yield. This is because the shorter time horizon means the principal repayment is less discounted. Furthermore, a bond with a shorter duration is, by definition, less volatile for a given yield change, as duration is the direct measure of this sensitivity.

Bond's holding period return, its duration, and the investment horizon- relationship

Holding Period Return =

$$\frac{Coupon\ payments + (End\ of\ Period\ Value - Initial\ Value)}{Initial\ Value}$$

The investment horizon is a critical factor in an investor's decision-making process. Short-term interest rate fluctuations are a significant concern for an investor who may need to sell a bond before maturity. In contrast, an investor with a long-term horizon is generally less concerned with short-term rate changes. While these fluctuations create unrealized gains or losses, the long-term investor is primarily focused on the total return over the entire investment period.

If interest rates rise, a buy-and-hold investor may ultimately see a higher total return. Although the bond's price will fall (as measured by duration), the investor can reinvest the coupon payments at the new, higher market rates. This increased reinvestment income can offset the initial price decline, especially as the bond's price is "pulled to par" at maturity. The opposite occurs when interest rates fall: the price appreciation is offset by lower reinvestment returns on coupons.

The interaction between holding period return, duration, and investment horizon can be summarized as follows:

- **When the investment horizon is longer than the bond's Macaulay duration:**
    - A **fall in interest rates** is generally detrimental. The benefit of higher bond prices is temporary and less impactful over a long horizon, while the lower reinvestment rate for coupons persists, reducing overall return.
    - A **rise in interest rates** is generally beneficial. The negative impact of the immediate price decline is muted over time, and the gain from reinvesting coupons at higher rates accrues over the long term, enhancing the total return.
- **When the investment horizon is shorter than the Macaulay duration,** the opposite relationships hold: rising rates hurt the total return, while falling rates help it.

When the investment horizon is precisely equal to the bond's Macaulay duration, the portfolio is immunized against interest rate risk. In this scenario, the capital loss from an immediate price change (due to a change in yield) is exactly offset by the gain from reinvesting coupon payments at the new rate, and vice versa. Consequently, the total return remains largely unaffected by the rate change.

The difference between the Macaulay duration and the investment horizon is known as the duration gap.

Duration Gap = Macaulay Duration – Investment Horizon

This gap measures the exposure to interest rate risk. A positive gap implies a position is vulnerable to rising rates, while a negative gap implies vulnerability to falling rates. The duration gap is not static; it evolves over time as the bond's duration changes and the investment horizon shortens.

Effect changes in credit spread and liquidity on yield-to-maturity

Yield to maturity = Benchmark rate + Spread-------- (1)

Benchmark rate = real rate of return or real rate of interest + expected inflation

Spread = credit risk + liquidity risk

So our equation (1) can be rewritten as

Yield to maturity = real rate of return or real rate of interest + expected inflation + credit risk + liquidity risk

The yield to maturity (YTM) of a bond can change due to shifts in the real risk-free rate, expected inflation, credit risk, or liquidity premiums. To estimate the impact of such a change on a bond's value, we can use the following formula, which incorporates both duration and convexity:

Change in Full Price ≈ – (Annual Modified Duration × ΔYTM) + [½ × Annual Convexity × (ΔYTM)²]

This formula provides a more accurate estimate than using duration alone, especially for larger yield changes.

If the change in YTM is not explicitly known, the change in the bond's credit spread (e.g., the Z-spread or G-spread) can often be used as a practical alternative for this calculation.

CHAPTER 6: FUNDAMENTALS OF CREDIT ANALYSIS

Credit risk, credit-related risks, default probability, and loss severity

Credit risk is the risk that a borrower will fail to make their scheduled interest and principal payments. It is composed of two key elements:

- **Default Risk (or Probability of Default):** This is the likelihood that a borrower will be unable or unwilling to pay their debt obligations on the due date.
- **Loss Severity (or Loss Given Default):** This refers to the portion of the asset's value that an investor will lose if a default occurs. It is often expressed as a percentage of the total exposure.

The overall **expected loss** from a loan or bond is calculated by combining these two components: Expected Loss = Probability of Default × Loss Severity.

Credit-Related Risks

Expected loss = Default risk × Loss severity

Recovery rate: The value of a security recovered after an issuer defaults. It can also be stated as the percentage of a bond's value an investor will receive upon default. (Note: Recovery Rate = 1 - Loss Severity).

Spread risk: The risk that a bond's credit spread will change due to a decline in the bond's liquidity or a deterioration in the issuer's creditworthiness. A fall in liquidity or creditworthiness causes the spread to increase.

Credit migration or downgrade risk: The risk that an issuer's creditworthiness will fall, leading to a lower credit rating.

Market liquidity risk: The risk that a bond's liquidity will decline, making it more difficult to buy or sell without affecting its price.

Seniority rankings of corporate debt and its limitations

The Debt Issued by Corporations

Corporate debt is ranked according to its priority of claims on the issuer's assets. Debt can be **secured** (backed by specific collateral) or **unsecured** (where the lender has a general claim on the issuer's

assets). Debentures are a common type of unsecured debt.
Secured debt has a higher priority claim on cash flows from assets than unsecured debt.

Secured debt can be further divided into first lien (or first mortgage), senior secured (or second lien), and junior secured. Unsecured debt is categorized as senior, junior, or subordinated. In the event of a default, unsecured debt claims are ranked below secured debt claims. The hierarchy of claims is generally as follows:

1. First lien / First mortgage
2. Senior secured / Second lien debt
3. Junior secured debt
4. Senior unsecured debt
5. Senior subordinated debt
6. Subordinated debt
7. Junior subordinated debt

All debts within the same category have equal priority, a principle known as *Pari Passu*.

If a firm defaults, the first debt to be paid is the first lien, with payments proceeding down the list. While this order is theoretically sound, it can be difficult to follow in practice. The default process is often costly and time-consuming. Debt holders who are not receiving their full claims may agree to a reorganization of payment priorities or debt terms (though the final decision typically rests with a court). In such cases, the strict seniority order may not be followed, and a junior class of debt may receive payment before a senior class.

Corporate issuer credit ratings and issue credit ratings and practice of "notching."

Credit rating agencies like Moody's, Standard & Poor's, and Fitch rate bonds based on the issuer's default risk. Bonds with similar credit risk are assigned comparable ratings. These agencies rate not only the corporations that issue the bonds but also the specific bond issues themselves.

The issuer's rating depends on its overall creditworthiness and is typically assessed using its senior unsecured bonds. The issuer's rating is called the Corporate Family Rating (CFR), while the rating for a specific bond issue is called the Corporate Credit Rating (CCR).

If one bond issued by a company is considered to be in default, it can trigger the default of other bonds from the same issuer. This mechanism is known as a **cross-default provision**.

The following are the rating scales assigned by the three most prominent agencies:

Investment rating		Non-investment rating	
S&P, Fitch	Moody's	S&P, Fitch	Moody's
AAA	Aaa	BB+	Ba1
AA+	Aa1	BB	Ba2
AA	Aa2	BB-	Ba3
AA-	Aa3	B+	B1
A+	A1	B	B2
A	A2	B-	B3
A-	A3	CCC+	Caa1
BBB+	Baa1	CCC	Caa2
BBB	Baa2	CCC-	Caa3
BBB-	Baa3	CC	Ca
		C	C
		D	

According to S&P and Fitch, the highest credit grade is AAA, while Moody's uses Aaa. Bonds rated from AAA (or Aaa) down to BBB- (or Baa3) are considered **investment-grade**. Bonds rated BB+ (or Ba1) and lower are categorized as **non-investment grade**, which are also commonly called high-yield, low-grade, or junk bonds.

An issuer can offer bonds with different maturities, coupon rates, and credit ratings. The process of assigning different credit ratings to various bonds issued by the same corporation is known as **"notching."** Notching is based on factors such as covenants, the bond's seniority within the capital structure, and its specific risk of default.

For example, a parent company and its subsidiary may both issue bonds. If the subsidiary's bond includes a provision (a covenant) that restricts it from transferring funds to the parent company until its own debt obligations are met, this can enhance the subsidiary's creditworthiness. As a result, the subsidiary's bonds could be assigned a higher credit rating than those of the parent company.

Risks in relying on credit rating agencies

While we can rely on ratings from credible agencies, it is important to recognize their limitations:

- **Ratings tend to lag the market:** Market prices adjust more quickly to new information than rating agencies can change their ratings. Therefore, prices often reflect changes in creditworthiness before the ratings are updated.

- **Rating agencies can make mistakes:** Although not a common occurrence, rating agencies are not infallible. They can occasionally assign a rating that is either mistakenly too high or too low.

- **Credit ratings change over time:** Ratings are not static; agencies adjust them from time to time based on an issuer's evolving financial health. Generally, higher-rated securities tend to be more stable, while lower-rated ones are more prone to change.

- **Some risks are difficult to quantify:** Certain risks are inherently challenging to model and incorporate into a rating. For example, litigation risks for industries like tobacco and alcohol are difficult to estimate fully. Similarly, the impact of natural calamities, such as earthquakes, is hard to predict with precision.

Four Cs of credit analysis

Traditional credit analysis is based on four key factors, often called the Four Cs: **Capacity, Collateral, Covenants, and Character.**

Capacity refers to the borrower's ability to repay its debt obligations. Analysis of capacity consists of three levels:

- **Industry Structure:** Analyzed using frameworks like Porter's Five Forces, which examines the threat of new entrants, the bargaining power of buyers and suppliers, the threat of substitute products, and the intensity of competitive rivalry within the industry.
- **Industry Fundamentals:** Involves examining key industry statistics, long-term growth prospects, and seasonal effects.
- **Company Fundamentals:** Focuses on the specific company's position within its industry, its historical financial record, and a detailed ratio analysis of its financial statements.

Collateral analysis is particularly important for firms with weaker credit profiles. It involves estimating the market value of the firm's assets that could be liquidated in case of default. Key factors considered include:

- **Intangible and Tangible Assets:** Tangible assets are typically easier to value than intangible assets. Some intangibles, like patents, can hold significant value as they can be sold. Others, like goodwill, are harder to value and may be written down if the company's performance deteriorates.

- **Depreciation:** If a company's depreciation expenses consistently exceed its capital expenditures, it may indicate insufficient investment to maintain its asset base.
- **Market vs. Book Value:** A company's stock trading below its book value per share can signal that the market believes its assets are overvalued on the balance sheet or are of low quality.

Covenants are the terms and conditions of a debt agreement designed to protect the lender. They can be affirmative (requiring specific actions) or negative (restricting certain activities). Excessively tight covenants can hinder a borrower's operational flexibility, potentially harming its ability to repay. Effective covenants should protect the lender's interests without unduly restricting the borrower's legitimate business activities.

Character refers to the quality and trustworthiness of a borrower's management team. This qualitative factor assesses the management's reputation, track record of honesty and ethical behavior, and their commitment to meeting financial obligations. It is often evaluated through interviews with management, reviews of their past business practices, and their overall standing in the business community.

Financial ratios used in credit analysis

Ratio analysis is a part of the capacity analysis of credit analysis. There are three major categories of ratios in credit analysis;

1. Profitability and cash flow ratios
2. Leverage ratios
3. Coverage ratios

Profitability and cash flow

EBITDA: Earnings before interest, taxes, depreciation, and amortization: This is the most commonly used metric to assess the credibility of a company.

EBIT = Operating income + depreciation + amortization

It assesses a company's financial performance by excluding the effects of depreciation, amortization, taxes, and interest. However, the exclusion of these items—particularly ongoing capital expenditures— is a primary limitation of ratios that use EBITDA. These necessary investments can significantly impact the amount of cash flow available to service debt, which is a critical concern for creditors.

Funds from operations (FFO): It is the net income from continuing operations + amortizations + Depreciation + deferred tax + other non-cash items. {FFO = EBITDA – changes in working capital}

Free cash flow before dividends: Net income depreciation + amortization - working capital - capital expenditures. More free flow before dividends, the better the creditworthiness of the company.

Free cash flow after dividends: This is equal to free cash flow before dividends – dividends

The higher the free cash flow after the dividends, the more funds are available for the creditors.

Leverage ratios

Debt to capital ratio= *Total debt / (debt + shareholder's equity)*

It shows the percentage of a company's capital that comes from debt. A lower (higher) ratio indicates greater (lower) creditworthiness and reduced (elevated) credit risk. A credit analyst must assess whether assets are overvalued, as this can make the ratio appear artificially attractive. Intangible assets, in particular, can be easily manipulated. In cases of overvaluation, the analyst must adjust the asset values before calculating this ratio.

***Debt to EBITDA** = Total debt /EBITDA:* A higher ratio indicates greater credit risk. Companies with volatile EBITDA—such as those in seasonal or cyclical industries—tend to have a highly volatile debt-to-EBITDA ratio.

FFO/Debt: **The FFO/Debt ratio measures credit health; a higher value corresponds to lower risk.**

Free Cash Flow after Dividends / Debt: A higher value for this ratio indicates **lower** credit risk.

Coverage Ratios

These ratios measure a borrower's ability to service its interest obligations.

- **EBITDA / Interest Expense:** A higher ratio indicates lower credit risk.
- **EBIT / Interest Expense:** A higher ratio indicates lower credit risk. This is a more conservative measure than the EBITDA/Interest Expense ratio because it excludes depreciation and amortization.

Factors that affect the yield spreads

We know that

Yield on a corporate bond = Real risk-free interest rate + Expected inflation rate + Maturity premium + Liquidity premium + Credit spread

And

Yield spread = Liquidity premium + Credit spread

Spread yield can be influenced by the following factors:

1. **Credit Cycle:** As the credit cycle improves, spreads narrow because the market perceives less credit risk. Conversely, spreads widen when the cycle deteriorates due to higher perceived risk.

2. **Economic Conditions:** Improved economic conditions lower perceived market risk, which leads to narrower spreads. The opposite is true in a deteriorating economy.

3. **Overall Financial Market Performance:** Efficient, well-performing, and less volatile financial markets generally lead to lower credit spreads.

4. **Broker/Dealer's Willingness:** Spreads narrow when brokers and dealers are willing to provide sufficient liquidity and capital for the bond market to function smoothly.
5. **Market Demand and Supply:** Spreads narrow during periods of high investor demand for bonds. They widen when the supply of new bonds exceeds market demand.

Things to consider when evaluating the credit of high-yield debt

High-Yield Debt

High-yield debt, also known as non-investment grade or "junk" bonds, is rated below Baa3 by Moody's or BBB by S&P/Fitch. These bonds receive lower ratings for the following reasons:

1. High leverage
2. Operation in a declining industry
3. Weak or limited operating history
4. High sensitivity to the business cycle
5. Lack of a durable competitive advantage
6. Poor quality management
7. Weak or negative cash flows
8. Significant off-balance-sheet liabilities

Due to their higher default risk, these bonds require special consideration through thorough due diligence on liquidity, financial projections, debt structure, corporate organization, and covenant strength.

Sovereign Debt

Sovereign bonds are issued by national governments. Bonds issued by the governments of developed countries are often considered risk-free. When analyzing these bonds, an analyst must focus on both the government's **ability** and its **willingness** to repay its debts. Key factors for assessing sovereign credit risk include:

1. **Institutional Effectiveness:** This refers to the government's competence in decision-making and policy implementation, as well as the prevalence of corruption within its institutions.
2. **Economic Growth Prospects:** The sustainability of economic growth, measured by trends in per-capita income, resource mobilization, and overall economic stability.
3. **International Position:** The nation's foreign exchange reserves levels, foreign direct investment, external debt burden, and exchange rate stability.
4. **Fiscal and Monetary Policy Flexibility:** The government's ability to generate revenue (e.g., by raising taxes) or reduce

expenditures. It also includes the central bank's capacity to implement effective and independent monetary policy.

Non-Sovereign Government Bonds

These bonds are issued by sub-national government entities. Unlike sovereign issuers, these entities do not have the authority to set monetary or fiscal policy.

That concludes our section on fixed-income securities. While we have taken diligent care in preparing this material, your honest feedback and comments are invaluable for future improvements.

You can also check out our other books on Investment and Evaluation, following the links

Financial Statements analysis

Derivatives and Alternative Investments

We also have books on the CFA Level One as follows

Financial Reporting and Analysis for CFA Level 1

Economics for Investment for CFA Level 1

Derivatives and Alternative Investments for CFA Level 1

Fixed Income for CFA Level 1

Equity investment for CFA Level 1